The
Storyteller

BY DARREN CARTER

ISBN: Softcover   978-1-5434-9468-6
        EBook   978-1-5434-9469-3

Print information available on the last page

Rev. date: 02/13/2019

To order additional copies of this book, contact:
Xlibris
0800-056-3182
www.xlibrispublishing.co.uk
Orders@ Xlibrispublishing.co.uk

The Storyteller

BY DARREN CARTER

The Demon Stigmata

&

The Daughters of the Eclipse

THE DEMON STIGMATA

The sky was red like blood.

Adrian's armour glistening in its fire.

His sword ready always for battle.

Adrian was chasing after destiny.

It led him to the mystery.

He came to the Mountains of the Red Mist.

A forbidden place.

Declared by Lord Lucifer,

That no demon may venture.

Adrian was thirsting for adventure.

It was the way to heaven.

Where the hearts of seven demons were taken.

Archangel Michael,

First showed his face.

In this barren place.

He took the hearts of the demons of fallen, disgrace.

+

Destiny was calling.

Adrian was resting.

He took some wine and gazed all around.

Hell would survive another war.

This time heaven will know the demons mighty roar.

Adrian began to climb the Mountain of the Red Mist.

A desire came over him.

Love would soon find its warrior.

At the summit,

He gazed at the unforgiving landscape.

Lost souls shall never escape.

+

Adrian settled himself behind a rock.

He laid his armour and sword by his side.

Then he closed his eyes to dream.

The sound of beauty disturbed Adrian from his sleep.

Adrian opened his eyes and love was born.

Two beautiful angels flying in the skies.

Love fired its bow.

Adrian's heart warmed to love.

Love came from heaven above.

One of the angels noticed Adrian.

She fell in love with this demon.

Closer they came.

Love wanted to know his name.

One angel descended from the red sky.

Her name was Diana.

Her beauty was like the Amir diamond.

Weakened demons by its desire.

+

Adrian and Diana,

Spoke tenderly to each other.

There was lover's hunger.

Each knowing their love was forbidden to their two worlds.

If their love was known.

They would lose both kingdoms for what they had done.

Diana called for another meeting.

Adrian agreed.

Tomorrow would be when love would believe.

Diana touched Adrian's cheek with love.

Diana returned to the skies.

Adrian waved his goodbyes.

Adrian gathered all his belongings and
headed down the mountain.

His world was now changing.

His holy desire will now be burning.

+

Climbing down from the Mountain of the Red Mist.

Adrian's thoughts weren't of war,

But of heavenly love.

A new war will soon wage within him.

For Adrian to be victorious.

His dreams will be beautiful.

Not of darkness.

But of loves true, pure light -

An angel of the Light.

+

Adrian started his journey back towards the Great Gate.

His heart was now free of all hate.

Love had made a home in his emptiness.

He felt the touch of perfect happiness.

In the distance his friend,

Alexander.

A demon warrior.

Adrian and Alexander knew of victory and honour.

They were in the campaign against the Cave Demons.

Where they took their final stand and claimed
a victory for their Demon clans.

But their time as a youth.

They spent it listening to the Great Maximillion.

Telling his war stories and of Demon legends.

+

Adrian and Alexander

Ordered the Great Gate to be opened.

The guards bowed to them as they were great.

Inside it was dark.

Torches shone the way.

The smell of pain and death lingered on the air.

Adrian saw the lost souls of despair.

They were being taken to the Pit of Sorrow for eternity.

Where the Demons wouldn't show them any pity.

One escaped his Demon guard and rushed towards Adrian.

Alexander stepped in line and drew his sword.

He brought the lost soul down.

Adrian knelt down to the man.

The man smiled as he saw the angels love in him.

He closed his eyes and his spirit left him.

+

Adrian's father came to meet them.

Atticus, an elder of Lucifer's council.

He knew there was looming a great battle.

Atticus told Adrian to go and visit his mother
Luna at the ruin Temple of Mirha.

It was close to the river of fear.

+

The ruin Temple of Mirha,

From the old days of worship.

It was where the Hiram rose grew.

It was honoured for its beauty.

It brought a Demon a good destiny.

Lord Lucifer destroyed the old ways.

With a strength of a thousand days.

He fired his evil power at its walls.

Its holy destiny would fall.

Adrian's mother, Luna.

Still kept the flames of prayer burning.

As she was not one of Lord Lucifer's following.

"My son you look troubled this night.

Come to me my delight."

Adrian prayed with his mother and reassured
her that all was well in his heart.

Then from the happiness of the moment.

Lord Lucifer's horns sounded.

Adrian had to leave.

His mother worshipped the flame of belief.

+

Adrian made his way to the Great Hall.

With the warm breeze on his face.

Like the touch of angel's wings.

His thoughts were of Diana.

Ahead of him were thousands of Demons.

Darkness will soon awaken.

Adrian looked up,

The red sky looked angry this night.

A storm was coming.

The two moons were rising.

Alexander met Adrian.

They followed the other Demons to the Temple of Lucifer.

To give him their honour.

They would make their way to the sanctuary
in front of the assembly of Demons.

+

Over the Bridge of Alames.

Towering over the Demon hoard.

Stood the statue of the Great Maximillon of old.

Every Demon touched him.

Believing that his great spirit would enter them.

Adrian wished he was still alive.

As he missed the stories he told.

Of times long ago.

When the kingdom was first born.

The Great Hall opened.

The Demons entered and marked themselves
with the blood of Lord Lucifer.

A mark of homage to their Lord.

Onwards to the Temple of Lucifer.

To give praise to the fallen Archangel.

+

Entering the Temple of Lucifer

The sound of the horns ceased.

Adrian and Alexander made their way to the front.

The gathering was beginning to be pleased.

As the Goddesses of Amyra were entering.

Beauty of evil.

Brought the gathering to an awakening.

With them came the hounds of hell,

With their blood red eyes.

Casting their gaze over the strong and the wise.

Amyra entered.

Her beauty brought Adrian to an evil surrender.

His eyes couldn't leave her sight.

This was a goddess for the night.

+

Lord Lucifer's angels descended from the red sky.

Wearing silver plated armour.

Ready to bring down heaven in the darkest hour.

Then silence came over assembly,

As the sound of great wings could be heard.

Then the Goddesses of Amyra began to sing.

Lord Lucifer descended.

The Demons and Adrian bowed in reverence.

Adrian thoughts were of his beautiful angel of deliverance.

Lord Lucifer walked to the Dark Bible.

To read a passage from the red angel.

His words soon turned to war.

The Demons broke the silence with a great roar.

The war of the Shadowlands will now begin.

Demons tonight,

it's for sin.

+

After the words of War echoed throughout the temple.

The darken angels sat on their marble thrones,

To witness Demon evil.

The goddesses of darkened pleasure.

Brought the kingdom to its measure.

Great evil was done under heaven this night.

Adrian longed for the goddess of the night.

Adrian left the temple with Amyra.

+

Adrian wished for dark love this night.

He followed her beautiful fragrance, to the fountain of dreams.

Amyra called for Adrian's unholy might.

He gave her his bodies blessings.

Adrian met his dark heaven.

He was truly lost in a sea of love.

+

Morning came.

The Demons rose from their night of evil shame.

The horns of War sounded.

They gathered their weapons.

Adrian woke from his dreams,

In the arms of beauty.

His love of the night.

Received his mark of strength and might.

Amyra had his honour.

She felt the longing of the ages.

Silence came after loves rages.

Adrian bestowed on her a kiss.

Amyra woke from her bliss.

A farewell was gifted to Adrian.

He was a warrior and love found a believer.

+

Warrior glory,

Opened its eyes from the dream of love.

Demons ready to honour Lord Lucifer from their sin.

Adrian remembered the promise to the angel Diana.

His heart called out for another gentle touch.

The beautiful angel of heaven with the gentle spirit.

Adrian in his father's armour.

Atticus was waiting to see the blood of his honour.

Adrian and Alexander

With glory and weapons in hand.

Their fathers giving them their faith and spirit.

Their mothers praying for Fate to bring them victory.

They got on their dark, black steeds.

To bring the Shadowlands to its knees.

The banner of Lord Lucifer was taken upon the wind.

The legions marched into legend.

+

Amyra from the tower,

Gazes at her lover.

Amyra's heart was taken.

Lord Lucifer had set is heart, on her.

The betrayal of love.

The heartbreak.

The Kingdom will feel the thunder and shake.

The crying of tears in the dark.

A warrior's love had left his mark.

The horns of war echoed across the kingdom.

The hounds of hell wished for evil freedom.

Lord Lucifer called to Amyra.

She turned.

She kept her true love hidden.

+

"Victory or death shall be ours,"

The Demons shouted.

Lord Lucifer,

Was in the arms of his beloved.

Across the forgotten wilderness,

The Demon legions singing songs of battles,

Victorious.

As they marched towards the end of their world.

Adrian and Alexander,

Leading the legions.

Forty thousand strong.

Their legend will live on.

Adrian looked up to the Mountain of the Red Mist.

His heart was touched by a beautiful angels last wish.

Adrian wondered if she was there,

Watching over him with her love and prayers.

+

Heaven came this day.

Diana's heart looked for her love.

Her eyes found joy.

Diana heard the sound of the horns of the Demons,

And saw Adrian ahead of the legions.

Her heart weakened.

Knowing her love was marching to war.

She couldn't live without him anymore.

Diana took to the skies.

And followed the love of her eyes.

Adrian marching to war.

Diana's love for him grew greater than before.

Heaven her kingdom was far away.

Diana followed for three days.

The legions came to rest at the pool of the whispering trees.

Adrian went to the pool to bathe,

From the long journey.

The angel saw his beauty.

+

Adrian,

Clothed himself with his battle armour.

His thoughts drifted away from the battle hour.

Towards the love of the air.

The angel with a heavenly stare.

Diana's love for Adrian,

Wanted to meet.

As she was rising from where she was hidden.

Alexander came,

The moment was taken.

Diana listened to the meeting.

Her loving heart beating.

When Adrian and Alexander parted.

Diana took to the air.

Her haven from this domain of fear.

+

Forbidden love never ending.

Was in the mind of Amyra.

She left Lord Lucifer's chamber.

Her heart of love was hoping,

That Adrian wasn't too far away.

As she needed his love for another day.

Amyra,

Went in search for her horse,

With darken wings.

She dreamed of waking in love with her chosen beloved.

Amyra,

Rode out into the wilderness.

To Adrian her lost happiness.

Lord Lucifer wakes.

**He goes to the window of his tower and
gazes at his love fleeing his honour.**

Lord Lucifer wondered where she was going at this hour.

He summoned a loyal dark angel to follow.

Lord Lucifer ordered him to return by tomorrow.

+

Dark love takes to the air.

Amyra would follow where love would take her.

Her darken winged horse,

Would smell the scent of demon.

She hoped for another secret moment with Adrian.

Night fell.

Adrian went back to the pool.

The night would be long.

The two red moons were full.

Adrian waited for the horizon of the day of war.

His heart desired love.

Amyra's darken winged horse flew in the sky.

With great strength.

The horse broke sweat.

Amyra demanded more.

The darken horse flew even faster and higher before.

Diana was asleep on a nearby hill.

Diana's love was strong like her will.

She dreamed of Adrian.

Her forbidden love.

Diana of heaven,

The angel of love.

Amyra came to the whispering woods.

She descended from the red sky of the two moons.

Amyra made her way to Adrian.

Not saying a word.

Silence of love was known.

As she started to show herself to her love lord.

Adrian's goddess of the night risked much to come.

As Lord Lucifer would share his throne and kingdom with her.

For the love of her darken freedom.

Adrian and Amyra embraced.

Bodies full of the desire of nature.

As the whispering woods whispered their names.

The wind took them to the sky,

Where Diana woke and cried.

+

The night was lost in the arms of love.

Amyra left as she came.

A forbidden dream.

The whispering trees whispered her name as
she disappeared into the darkness.

Amyra took to the sky

And started her journey back to Lord Lucifer.

Her love for Adrian grew stronger.

She hoped and dreamed to see Adrian again.

Diana's tears,

Like the river of forever.

Her holy love dying.

But her heart was strong.

Adrian laid awake waiting for the morning horn.

He thought of his legions.

The spirit of the heart of every Demon.

The dark angel,

Heard and saw.

He took witness and he would break this hidden secret.

+

The destiny of war awaits those of a brave spirit.

Let songs and legends be written of these Demon warriors,

Of axe, sword and spear.

Let them live forever.

Adrian heard the morning horn

and ordered all the Demons to gather to
hear their heart of the legions speak.

"It is for now we live.

Let it bring us victory.

As we go towards our destiny, with axe, sword and spear;

Let the dark angels hear our battle cries,

And take our victory to Lord Lucifer.

The dead, let them always be remembered,

And the living honoured."

+

The hidden secret was revealed.

The dark angel told Lord Lucifer of the whispering trees.

The knowledge of their whispers brought

Lord Lucifer to his knees.

Anger is born in his eyes.

Amyra will feel his rage.

As the evil sun rises.

Amyra arrived too late,

to save her from her fate.

She reaches the Lord Lucifer's chamber

and sees her lord waiting for her.

The dark angel watching from behind

a pillar within the darkness.

Waiting to hear her screams.

Amyra came closer.

Lord Lucifer struck her down.

Amyra looked up with tears in her eyes.

Lord Lucifer's heart full of love,

Turned quickly to anger.

He felt the touch of betrayal.

Amyra offered herself as a sacrifice.

she took Lord Lucifer into the night.

The dark angel left and took flight.

In the morning light.

+

The angel watches Adrian.

She dreams of a new kingdom from the spirit of her love.

Adrian gives the order.

The Demon legions march onwards.

By the end of this day they would have reached their end.

The Shadowlands.

The angel Diana would watch from the
skies and from the rocks.

Adrian's life and world, belonged to her now.

The cup of destiny was theirs to share and behold.

+

The Battle of the Shadowlands.

Legions of thousands.

Demons cheering.

Demons roaring.

With their war banners,

Horns sounding.

Axes, swords and spears,

Held up to the red sky.

Adrian was ready to live or die.

Adrian took a moment to touch his breast plate and
think of his father and his beloved mother.

Adrian thought of the Great Maximillion.

He was going to give his kingdom glory and a great victory.

The order was given by Alexander.

The demons moved into the demon head formation for battle.

To kill for the red angel.

Silence fell over this unforgiving land.

As they waited for the Shadow Demons to appear.

From the distance their horns could be heard.

Adrian turned to Alexander and said,

"Our destiny is here."

+

The greatest of all battles,

Where much blood would be spilt and
death will bring the final honour.

Was waiting to begin.

Diana heard the final horn sound.

The ground shook and the thunder brought the Angel of Death.

The battle was fierce.

The red dust drenched in Demon blood.

Again, and again,

The Demons fought.

Destiny fell.

Warrior Demons died.

But the battle waged on.

Ground was taken,

Then lost.

Adrian's demons with a great desire for blood came forward.

Adrian showing his brave heart.

Slaying Shadow Demons to his left and to his right.

The legions of Adrian,
Took belief in their heart.
they would follow him to the ends of hell.

Diana saw her love in battle.
She saw his fire.
That brought her love to wonder.

Adrian wasn't afraid of the fear of death.
He was born for this.
He loved the kill.
The more he killed,
The more he wanted to feel the kill on his steel.

As evening, was closing in.
The battle turned.
Adrian the brave heart,
Was separated from his loyal Demons.

The desire for blood.
The fire inside took him away.

Adrian was lost to the blood rage.

Death was being summoned.

From out of the darkness.

Destiny felt the spear of death.

Adrian fell.

The spear pierced his armour.

His heart was beating his last.

Diana couldn't let her love past.

Alexander witnessed the tragedy.

He charged on his darken steed,

But he couldn't reach his friend.

Alexander felt the pain of lost.

Adrian's life would be victories cost.

As Adrian began to see the darkness
of death in front of his eyes.

His last thoughts were of his angel of love.

From the skies Diana saw the tragedy awakening.

When the Shadow Demons were finally vanquished,

And thousands were taken as prisoners.

Diana came from the skies and knelt by the love of her life.

She called out his name.

Adrian heard her sweet voice,

from out of the darkness of death,

Calling him back.

With her open wings and her sweet voice.

She prayed,

And bestowed on Adrian the gift.

It came as swift as a holy Dove.

A gift from heaven.

His life entered his body was more.

The only way Diana knew to beat death.

As every angel is touched by the Saviour.

When they heal a Demon.

you receive the Stigmata.

It is written in the unholy book.

That one will come to destroy and build.

To regain his kingdom,

which was lost,

From one of heavenly, love.

+

Demons in mourning.

The new day was darkening.

Alexander with sadness

Weighing down on his heart,

Brought the legions and what was left of the
Shadow Demons back to their kingdom.

Without rest,

The Demons marched west.

Knowing their victory,

Came with a great price,

Their brave beating heart;

The bringer of death

Brought this tragedy.

The kingdom they knew had lost a
brave Demon to their destiny.

Entering the Great Gate.

Lord Lucifer was waiting and hoping.

An honoured guard with armour shining.

Noticed many of their Demon hood were missing,

And their brave heart not beating.

Amyra saw Adrian's absence.

Amyra felt the veil of sadness.

Lord Lucifer was told of the lost.

Adrian's father comforted his wife.

Luna wished death would take her life.

+

The Demon Stigmata rises from the ashes.

Like a darken Phoenix.

The strength of the beauty of love willed it.

Adrian opened his eyes and saw the
beauty of heaven looking back.

Diana created the Holy Pact.

Adrian felt the pain of the nails in his palms.

He felt the crown of thorns.

Adrian turned to Diana and asked her what it meant.

Then he felt the nails in his feet,

And he wept.

Diana spoke,

"You now feel the love of my kind.

The Saviour who was crucified.

Come with me now,

Return back to your family."

+

The curse in the eyes of the Demons.

Diana brought back to the fold.

Diana watched from a distance as Adrian

announced himself at the Great Gate.

Adrian heard the sound of the mourning horn,

Honouring the brave fallen.

Adrian was still a brave warrior Demon.

But within heaven had found a new haven.

The guards on the Great Gate,

Couldn't believe their eyes.

One rushed to the gathering to tell them that

Adrian had returned from the angel of death.

The other guard fell to the ground,

Thinking he was seeing a ghost.

Till Adrian opened his mouth and spoke.

+

The words of Adrian were of heaven.

The guard allowed him in.

Adrian sensed a kingdom of great sin.

Demons on every side,

sensed one thing,

And thought another.

Till one shouted,

"The angel Saviour."

Adrian rushed to his father.

Atticus was ashamed,

That his son is known under a forbidden name.

His mother wanted to show Adrian her love.

But Atticus denied the touch.

The Demon Prophet Talus,

Rushed to Lord Lucifer.

"Here is the curse.

The end is in your sight.

The Demon Stigmata has returned to life."

Amyra begged for mercy for Adrian.

The prize would be her hand in love.

Lord Lucifer ordered Adrian,

To be taken to the darkest dungeon.

Lord Lucifer thought of killing Adrian
with the three headed Dragon.

+

The dungeon was dark,

With the presence of evil.

Adrian felt alone.

He was chained in this dark prison.

He dreamed of being risen.

Adrian had lost his world but gained heaven.

He longed to see Diana again.

His heart would forever burn for her name.

Hours and hours went by.

Days began and ended.

Adrian waited for a sign.

He heard voices.

His soul felt wounded.

The door to his cell opened.

The goddess of the night entered,

Amyra.

She sensed Adrian was touched by the light.

She was still in love with the sight.

Amyra touched Adrian,

And spoke words of never-ending love.

Then Adrian sensed heaven returning.

A light appeared,

There was Diana.

Adrian at that moment,

Feels the wrath of the whip.

He feels holy pain.

Which burns the origin of his name;

+

The goddess of his love of the night and
the angel of love of his morning,
Were both before him.

Two beautiful temples of love.
Both seeking to hold onto Adrian's heart.
Amyra and Diana looked at Adrian,
With love in their eyes.
Destiny had two beating hearts for Adrian.
A forbidden triangle of love.

"I needed to see you again Diana," declared Adrian.
"I will always be here," replied Diana.
With the arrow of love piercing her heart.

The darkness of jealousy took Amyra.

"She is the one who helped you regain
your soul?" asked Amyra.

Adrian felt heavenly, beauty and wonder for Diana.
Amyra left.
Hate for the both of them grew inside her.

+

Lord Lucifer passed sentenced in the morning.

All gathered and so did Adrian's kin.

The sentence being execution by the three headed Dragon.

Demon guards were ordered to take Adrian to his death.

Diana heard danger, coming.

She disappeared in the light of heaven.

The Demon guards took Adrian to the place of execution.

Lord Lucifer would leave it to evil, Fate.

Inside him was great hate.

Amyra love for Adrian was fading.

Her flame of love being taken by the darkness of jealousy.

She wished Adrian not to have a Saviour.

Adrian was placed in the Three headed Dragons den.

The door was locked.

The Demons wished for death.

The three headed Dragon came,

Following the Demons scent.

Then Diana came,

Heaven sent.

She put the Dragon to sleep.

Adrian was safe and waited for the morning.

Diana stayed till the evil sun was rising.

+

Lord Lucifer came to the den and saw
his beloved Dragon sleeping.

And Adrian awake and kneeling.

The evil rage inside Lord Lucifer began to be heated.

When his desire of death went unanswered.

Fate ignored his request,

And brought life instead.

Lord Lucifer gave orders to take Adrian to the Pit of Sorrow.

Time went by.

Adrian worked in the pit.

The Demons cast lots to see how long he would live.

Then one day Amyra came.

She saw Adrian working in the pit.

She still denied her love for him and
ordered him to be whipped.

The darken love grew in her eyes.

As love became as hot as the sun rise.

Amyra called Adrian over to her.

She touched his beauty.

It was still her hidden destiny.

Amyra touched his face.

Adrian only felt,

Diana's touch of heavenly grace.

Diana was still with him in spirit.

She gave him the strength to carry it.

+

The sands of time ran for Adrian.

He suffered.

Then Lord Lucifer ordered,

That Adrian would be taken back to his cell.

Where the love of Amyra and Lord Lucifer
would tempt Adrian's soul to leave,
And bring Adrian back to his dark beliefs.

Time of their embraces never ended.
Adrian never looked up and saw their faces.
The Goddesses of Amyra came with their desires.
To seduce Adrian's raging fires.

Adrian closed his eyes and only heard,
Diana's voice.
She was stronger than the evil force.

Lord Lucifer was enraged again.
How would this story end;

The end did come by Lord Lucifer command.
Adrian was led to the archery arena.
Where he would die as a Demon warrior,
After the pleadings by his father.

Adrian was tied to a post.
His families love for him returned.

His father saw his son's bravery.

He knew then that this heavenly love was worthy.

Adrian's chest was shown.

The Demon archers prepared their bows.

Adrian looked up to heaven.

Diana was flying in the red skies,

Knowing her love was going to die.

The archers fired arrow after arrow.

They all found their mark.

The final sign,

An arrow like the spear,

Entering his side.

Adrian felt his holy soul rise.

Adrian died.

The darkness reclaimed his spirit.

When night, came.

His family and Alexander came to take his body.

They hid it in secret.

At the ruin Temple of Mirha.

Diana watched and followed.

When silence came and the darkness of the night.
Diana came to be with her Adrian.

Diana had lost her kingdom.
Forever she would tend to Adrian's grave,
With loving tenderness.
Till God's forgiveness.

+++

THE DAUGHTERS OF THE ECLIPSE

In the darkness of the night.
The creatures of the night,
Watch as the moon rises from its sleep.
Into the heavens where angels weep.

In a town, there is silence.
As good daughters sleep with Orpheus.
But some wait for the call.
When the moon is full.
To go to the castle by the cliffs.

The daughters of the eclipse will come.
They will be taken over by the moon.
They will raise their hands to the dark sky,
To receive the moons power and praise.

The stone altar of delight.
Where they will show their honour.

The goddess of the moon,

Will bestow on each a gift of power.

They will receive it at the bewitching hour.

(

A new family enters the town.

They have a daughter called Sarah.

Who catches the sight of one young man;

A Mechanic called Sam.

Sarah's family arrive at their new home.

They see an old woman.

They unpack and settle in.

Sarah's mother is a Christian.

She places a crucifix on the wall,

but it falls onto the floor.

Sarah's father picks up the crucifix.

"Don't worry,

It's only a coincidence.

There isn't an evil presence."

Sarah's father works in the city.

He's is an architect.

He comes home late.

Sarah doesn't see him much during the week.

As when he comes home,

Sarah is fast asleep.

Across the street,

Is a closed church.

Sarah's mother is looking for work.

(

First day at the High School.

Sarah walks down the lane.

She sees the old woman again.

Sarah senses her eyes on her.

Which makes Sarah have fear.

"Hello dear."

The old woman speaks.

Sarah waves.

Sarah wishes she was safe.

Since Sarah could remember.

She has had a strange dream.

It is of her walking naked by a stream.

It is at night.

The full moon is bright.

She goes to the cliffs and gazes down.

Where she falls and drowns.

She only believes it to be a bad dream.

But with the crucifix falling to the floor.

Sarah begins to think,

What it really means for her.

When she reaches High School.

Sarah sees two girls Catherine and Allison.

They are fans of the rock band Red Satan.

Sarah says hello.

As the two girls are listening to a track called Dark Halo.

Sarah laughs at the thought.

Her mother would be shocked.

(

New friendships begin.

Later, there will be sin.

The bell rings.

The school day begins.

Sarah follows her new friends.

They show her the way.

English Literature,

Is the first class of the day.

The teacher reads a poem from a local poet.

Catherine and Allison enjoy it.

She reads a poem about the castle on the cliffs.

Sarah looks out of the classroom window,

And across the street,

is the old woman standing there;

Shaking her head in despair.

What does it all mean,

Sarah wonders in a daydream.

(

The day carries on.

Sarah is having fun,

With her new friends,

Catherine and Allison.

They go to Allison's, locker.

She looks in her mirror.

She is a looker.

All the boys are after her.

She teases them rotten.

Catherine is the bad one.

She has a locket around her neck,

Its silver.

It's been in her family,

ever since they first moved to Moon River.

Catherine and Allison's families have lived
in Moon River for centuries.

The old woman knows all the local legends and stories.

The final lesson of the day,

Is Music.

Sarah has always loved singing.

When the singing begins,

She gets lost within the lesson.

Sarah feels she has lost her will and reason.

Her friends,

The other girls

And the female teacher.

They sing strangely.

It makes Sarah drift away.

The rest of the girls and the female teacher begin to sway.

The boys seem to be in a trance.

The girls and the female teacher begin to dance.

Sarah feels the music in her mind.

She feels the freedom of a bird flying upon the wind.

Then they are brought back to reality.

By the sound of the bell,

Everything is now well.

(

Home time is here.

Sarah invites friendship home, with her.

The journey home is full of laughter,

And talking about music and boys.

What stories were told.

Then they catch sight of Sam in the garage.

He's working on a vintage Rolls Royce.

He works sometimes late.

The girls always ask him for a date.

Sarah is a bit shy.

Sam thinks she has beautiful eyes.

The girls leave.

Sarah looks back to Sam working on the car.

She likes the idea of a tall, dark handsome stranger.

Sam has Sarah on his mind.

Sam thinks her heart is kind.

But he has work, to do.

He doesn't want to work too late,

As he is going out with his mates.

(

Arriving home.

They go past the old woman.

She's out in her garden,

With her black cat.

Tending to her flowers,

It was a dark hour.

The old woman is acting strange,

She doesn't say anything at all.

The old woman is stroking her cat,

Who is sitting on the wall;

Catherine and Allison give the woman an evil stare.

The woman looks at her cat,

Who arches her back;

The cat starts to walk on the wall, hissing.

Catherine and Allison tell Sarah,

That the old woman gazes into a crystal ball at night,

By candle light.

They also tell Sarah,

they wish she would go away.

That would be a happy day.

(

"I'm home," shouts Sarah.

Sarah sees her mother.

Sarah sees she is a lot happier.

Sarah asks her "Why"

Her mother cuts a piece of apple pie.

"I've got a job at your school, as a cleaner.

Are you pleased?"

Sarah doesn't like the idea.

As she likes her own space.

With her mother working at school,

The other students will laugh at her face.

"I've brought two friend's home,

Catherine and Allison," says Sarah.

When Sarah's mother sees them,

she is pleased.

But not what she sees.

Their T- Shirts of Red Satan.

Upsets Sarah's mother as she is a devote Christian.

"I hope they are not going to teach you bad things," replies Sarah's mother.

"Mother! I've had a long day.

I'm taking Catherine and Allison to my bedroom for a while," says Sarah.

(

It is a hot day.

Sarah's mother left the window open.

Sarah sees the old woman.

The old woman nods her head.

Catherine and Allison sit on the bed.

They call to Sarah.

Sarah turns.

Catherine says,

"I wish that old, woman burns."

Sarah is shocked with what she hears.

Catherine smiles.

"It's only a joke.

Don't take it seriously."

"Catherine always says things which are silly,"

Replies Allison.

Catherine shows Sarah her locket.
Sarah likes the look of it.

Allison leaves Catherine alone with Sarah.
Allison leaves the house,
As quiet as a mouse.

Catherine starts swinging the locket gently.
Chanting words only Catherine and Allison know.

Catherine starts to chant an ancient rhyme.
Sarah loses all track of, time.

Catherine tells Sarah to lay down.
As Allison sees Sam heading back to town.
Sarah enters a deep sleep,
But she sees Allison rushing down the street.

Sarah sees Allison heading towards Sam in the garage.
Sarah hears Allison begin to sing and she rubs her ring.
Sam begins to go into a trance.
Allison begins to show herself and she begins to dance.

Sarah cries out no,

And she begins to move on her bed.

Catherine wishes the old woman to be dead.

Sarah sees Allison come closer to Sam.

As darken love comes over them.

Sarah cries tears of lost love this day.

Sarah wishes she could run away.

Catherine leaves Sarah on her bed in tears.

Sarah will remember this dream for years.

Catherine knocks the crucifix down onto the floor.

Catherine only loves Satan and nothing more.

(

Sarah leaves her room and wipes her eyes.

She goes down stairs,

to see the evils surprise.

The crucifix fallen on to the floor.

Sarah feels anger like never before.

Her mother sees the scene,

and she orders Sarah not to leave.

Sarah's mother,

Orders Sarah to put the crucifix back on to the wall.

Sarah throws it like a ball.

Sarah storms out of the house in great anger,

And sits on the grass.

The old woman is with her black cat.

Sarah's mother leaves and tells Sarah she is not pleased.

"I must go to work now Sarah. We will talk about
this later," Sarah mother says angerly.

Sarah's mother drives away.

Sarah is not happy this day.

The old woman calls Sarah to come over.

Sarah anger hides her fear.

The first meeting.

Sarah has been waiting for.

She can't wait to see inside her house.

The old woman's house has many pictures on the walls.
Sarah see her crystal ball.

The old woman has a library of books.
Sarah would love to take a look.
Sarah see's the books.
Some are of Astrology,
Others were of witchcraft,
There were some of Ancient History,
all have a sense of mystery.
There were some first editions and books on
natural remedies to cure all human ills.
Sarah felt the room to be free of evils.

"Would you like a cup of tea,"
Asks the old woman.
Sarah nods in agreement.
Sarah was lost in the moment.

Hours go by.
Sarah listens to the old woman.
She tells stories of legends.
She tells stories of Moon River.

Of a beautiful girl who once lost her will because of fear.

She loses her mind,

Because of the evil kind.

Now they hate her.

As she has never grown up.

She is still a young girl,

an innocent of the world.

Sarah understands the girl is the old woman.

What did she experience and where?

Sarah wanted to know.

It will explain everything and her dream.

She dreams every night,

Which gives her a fright.

"It happened by the cliffs by the castle.

I was so beautiful and gentle," says the old woman.

Sarah sees a photo of her on the mantle.

The old woman carries on,

"The daughters of the eclipse gather there at the full moon.

It will be soon.

You must leave here.

It will only bring you the curse of fear."

(

As Sarah leaves,

She takes another look at the picture on the mantle.

the old woman was truly very beautiful.

Sarah knows she must leave.

As her mother will be returning.

She enjoyed her meeting.

She learnt a lot.

(

Sarah's mother returns from work.

Ready to give Sarah a talk.

Sarah is sitting on the sofa.

Sarah's mother still loves her.

They sit together,

Sharing what was the matter.

Sarah's mother,

Understands the love tears of rain.

Sarah promises it won't happen again.

Sarah kisses her mother goodnight.

Her mother is pleased that her daughter is alright.

Sarah goes to her bedroom.

Where her darken, dream will loom.

Then night comes to end the day.

But danger, stays.

Catherine has witnessed the events of the day and night,

Under the moonlight.

(

The household is asleep.

Sarah begins to dream,

Her nightmare hides within.

The moon is full.

The eclipse has come.

The daughters of the eclipse leave their homes.

They are like nature,

Wild and free.

Their skin feels the breeze.

From the north,

From the south,

From the east,

From the west,

They come.

To give, honour.

To the Goddess of the moon.

The castle by the cliffs,

Looks over the gathering.

All the daughters are chanting.

Far into the night.

They dance free,

Around the altar of delight.

Where a sacrifice will take place.

A man who would hide his face.

A ship is witnessed from the rocks.

They sing their evil chorus.

A sacrifice fitting for the goddess will be selected.

One who the women will all be delighted.

Sarah begins to sing,

With the daughters of the eclipse.

The ship rest on the rocks.

the daughters look.

They have such beauty.

It will bring the men to their final destiny.

The daughters from the rocks.

They go out to the wreck of the ship.

Which lies in the dark;

Sarah feels the silence.

Then the screams are heard.

It is of men young and old.

The daughters return with their prize.

A delight for their eyes.

A man,

A sailor.

Who would be surrendered,

The goddess of the moon will be honoured.

The daughters bring the sailor to the altar of delight.

The daughters prepare him for the darken night.

They all dance,

In praise and honour.

As the goddess of the moon appears,

In gold and splendour.

The sailor is in a trance.

The daughters begin their dance.

The goddess touches the sailor

With her body.

She wishes to have his life energy.

The goddess of the moon,

Touches his cheek and kisses him with the kiss of death.

The daughters catch their breath.

Sarah wakes and cries.

She now knows the secret of the past.

Will she now last.

(

The new day has come.

The days of rest, are here.

Sarah knows the cliffs hold the answer.

She looks at the calendar,

And sees the eclipse is two days away.

That will be her destiny day.

She comes downstairs and tells her mother she is going out.

Sarah's mother is happy she is up and about.

Her father,

Waves her goodbye and wishes her safe.

Sarah walks away,

As she wants to be by herself.

On her way,

Sam is there.

He offers to take her to the cliffs.

He will remain to keep her safe.

They talk together on the journey.

Sam reveals his love for Sarah and
convinces her she is the only one.

Sarah feels the heat of the sun.

(

Closer Sarah comes to this begotten place,

She feels the evil on her face.

Sam is talking,

But to Sarah it's only a distant whisper.

Sarah is lost.

Her soul takes flight.

She feels like a daughter in the darken night.

Sarah leaves Sam behind and walks to the Altar.

There are faces within the stone,

Of men in pain and anguish.

Their eyes are closed and hidden to the world.

Their life is taken.

**On the breeze Sarah hears centuries of daughters
chanting and singing their ancient curse.**

Sarah begins to see their spirits dancing to the evil verse.

For men to fall prey to their want and need.

It will be the time to make all men bleed.

Sarah hears the water crashing against the rocks of stone.

Sarah is finally at home.

Sarah faith of her mother leaves and a new belief lives.

This is her true calling.

Now she feels she is falling,

Under the darken gaze of the castle.

Sarah begins to sing and dance.

With the centuries of daughters of long ago.

She feels the power which she knows.

(

Sarah comes to Sam,

With darken love in her heart.

The place has taken over her.

The spirits of the daughters of the eclipse have entered her.

Sarah sees with the eyes of a ghost.

Lost to love.

But with a great thirst.

Sarah feels all the power of nature and the universe in her body.

Sarah feels the kingdom of the daughters.

The spirits wish to take Sam to the slaughter.

Sam is fighting the trance.

Sam makes his stand.

He calls to Sarah to stop and return.

Sarah darken love begins to burn.

Sam backs away towards the cliffs.

Sarah loses herself.

She comes slowly forward.

Sam enters the trance.

Sarah face changes to a face of evil.

Sarah has lost all of her will.

Sam falls to the rocks below.

The unforgiving sea receives his spirit.

(

When Sarah got home and she was walking up the drive.

There was a car,

Which captured her eyes.

It was the one from her dream that day.

Where Allison took her lover's dream away.

A vintage Rolls Royce.

Shining in the light.

It had a red moon of the night.

Entering the house,

She heard voices.

They were of beauty,

Voices which will lead her to destiny.

"Sarah.

This is Jennifer and Vivienne.

They are Catherine and Allison's mothers.

Come and greet them,

They've been waiting," says Sarah's mother.

Sarah was told of the sad news of the old woman.

She had disappeared,

During the night.

Sarah will never see her sight.

Now the daughters are complete again.

Sarah is the one.

Now the daughters can dance around the altar of stone.

To bring men down to their bidding.

They will receive the power,

which was theirs since the beginning.

Jennifer, gave Sarah a bracelet,

Which held her power.

Now she will await the eclipse hour.

(

Night was falling.

The spirits at the cliffs were calling.

Jennifer and Vivienne were leaving.

They invited Sarah to a gathering at the mansion.

The car would pick her up.

Driven by the Groundsman.

But before they left.

They saw Christ on the Cross.

They looked and smiled,

What a sacrifice that would cost.

"Are you Catholics?"

Asked Sarah's mother.

"No!

We believe in the ancient ways.

When the world was first born.

Where there was the goddess of the moon," replied Vivienne.

Sarah's mother didn't understand the words they spoke.

Sarah's mother smiled as she believed in the Holy Ghost.

Sarah's mother tells Sarah that some young
men are missing from the town this day.

No one knows if they've gone away,

And Sam's, body was found on the beach,

He had sea-weed wrapped around his feet.

(

The gathering of the cliffs.

The eve of the eclipse.

The daughters of the eclipse come.

as many as the hours of a clock.

The ancient breeze leads them to the unholy place.

They have beauty upon their faces.

The stars of the night sky,

Lighten their eyes.

Sarah is amongst them.

She has the fire within her.

Her beating heart of, fire,

Will be calmed by her desire.

The night is young.

The daughters of the eclipse have come.

They wait for the moment of darken love.

A moment they've been waiting for.

Their hunger has been calling them
darker and stronger than before.

The men are released from the cell beneath the castle walls.

Their doom has followed their destiny to their fall.

The daughters begin to sing and dance.

The men fall into a trance.

To the altar of delight.

The young men's beauty is shown to the night.

The daughters of the eclipse begin their darken love.

Watched by the light of the moon above.

The screams are heard from within the darkness.

Their bodies are given to the unforgiving sea.

(

Sarah returned to her home and waited for destiny,

to call.

She looked at her bracelet.

There was a moon engraved.

A symbol of the power she craved.

As she touched it,

she felt it's power.

It was passed the bewitching hour.

The dawn came,

Destiny was calling Sarah's name.

The Rolls Royce arrived at Sarah's house.

Sarah saw the Groundsman.

Young and strong.

The darken love will last all night long.

The night will be taken away.

Sarah will lose a day.

The Groundsman took Sarah to the mansion.

It was out of town.

Through an open gate,

With two stone ravens,

Watch and wait.

The trees of darkness,

Showed Sarah the way to the mansion of stone.

Sarah sensed it's darken-tale.

Where the daughters of the eclipse always dwelled.

Jennifer and Vivienne were waiting.

Catherine and Allison were on the balcony,

Gazing at the sight of lover's destiny.

Sarah got out from the car and went
inside the mansion of stone.

What wonders would be shown.

The Groundsman attended to the car.
Catherine and Allison gazed from afar.

There were others there,
Gazing out from the window.
Their beauty shone,
Like the new dawn of a new tomorrow.

They were whispering about the Groundsman.
Their bodies were beginning to dance.
Sarah took a second glance.

Jennifer and Vivienne,
Showed Sarah the Great Hall.
Where there was a table with ancient carvings,
Chairs and a marble floor.

Around the walls were paintings of
past daughters of the eclipse.
Sarah was still feeling the dance.
She was desiring evil to touch her lips.
There she saw the statue in marble of the goddess of the moon.
She was very beautiful and powerful.

A goddess of the ancient ways.
Her power would last a thousand days.

The other daughters returned.
They were of great beauty.
Waiting for the daughter of destiny.

Jennifer lead the daughters in a prayerful chant.
To honour the goddess of the moon.

Then Catherine and Allison brought in the Groundsman
Into the Great Hall.
(
As he entered,
The daughters left one by one,
touching his body.
Sarah was alone,
With the spirits to keep her company.

From outside the chant of evil prayer was heard.
Sarah began to feel the freedom of a bird.

The Groundsman turned to the paintings on the wall.

The spirits escaped and flew around the room.

Whispering words of desire, lust and of evil.

Wishing Sarah to have her awakening.

While the spirits would be feeling.

Sarah time was beginning.

The spirits took the Groundsman to
the table and held him down.

Sarah awakening began.

Evil,

Dark love,

Ran through her body.

She felt the Groundsman energy.

The daughters of the eclipse felt the dark feeling,

As the moon was rising.

The daughters of the eclipse,

Felt the spirits of the daughters of the centuries.

The doors to the Great Hall opened.

Sarah held the hand of the Groundsman,

And the daughters of the eclipse followed.

Chanting praise,

To the daughter of their days.

To the cliffs they went.

The man in a dream.

The daughters of the eclipse desiring their promised power.

As the clock in the tower tolled the hour.

As the moon became one.

The daughters of the eclipse placed the
Groundsman on the altar of stone.

The daughters of the eclipse danced,

Under the moonlight.

The coming came.

The eclipse shone,

With rays of light.

The daughters of the eclipse felt delight.

The goddess appeared.

The goddess of ancient power,

this was the goddesses, hour.

The goddess took the man's breath with desires might.

The goddess stood up and gave her promise of power.

The daughters of the eclipse felt the evil surrender.

The Groundsman was pushed off the
cliffs into the watery depths.

The goddess disappeared after the death.

The daughters of the eclipse disappeared within the darkness.

Sarah was left alone.

but she felt a touch.

The old woman's black cat showing love.

They both walked to the cliff edge,

and gazed into the dark, cold waters.

Sarah was now a true daughter.

*(